The Poetry Book Society
Anthology 1986/87

"ANOTHER SLIM VOLUME OF MODERN
ENGLISH POETRY!" SHRIEKED JACOBSEN

GLEN BAXTER

Contents

5

Introduction

Glen Baxter's marvellous frontispiece first appeared in 1979 and serves as a reminder that until quite recently English poetry had a poor public image, especially among those like Jacobsen who did not read it. Poetry was not only supposed to be unbearably dull and irrelevant; it was also popularly seen as a cerebral and obscure linguistic game written by and for people far cleverer than you or I. Both these views (perhaps fostered by memories of joylessly learning "Cargoes" by rote on overcast afternoons at school) are hopelessly wrong as the poems you are about to read demonstrate.

This is the first time the Poetry Book Society annual anthology of new poems – which has appeared now for thirty years – has been so substantial and also available to non-members of the Society. I was delighted to be invited to edit this year's, but I have not attempted to be truly representative. For one thing, poetry today is so various that I should need even more pages to do that. For another, not every poet to whom I wrote had new work available to send. So what I have attempted to present is a personal selection of new work by some of our best poets. But first I should like to mention the part played by Philip Larkin in reinvigorating the role of the Poetry Book Society. He died in 1985, a few months after Eric W. White, who virtually founded the Society. It was Philip who, when Chairman, suggested that books of new poetry be offered to members at *discount*; a major change of policy which he also guided deftly through committee with his characteristic blend of patience, tough-mindedness and dry wit. Philip liked to inject humour into serious proceedings (I imagine along the lines of T. S. Eliot setting off firecrackers at Faber board meetings); and it is his sense of humour I recollect most vividly from that time of apparently endless meetings. In contrast, though, I value most those of his poems which are sensitive and serious, and I reprint four here first published between 1951–1977 in various places, but each previously uncollected.

Philip Larkin was not the only loss to poetry in the past year. Geoffrey Grigson who, although he produced his best poems in his last eight years, always remained better known as a critic and anthologist; Christopher Isherwood, primarily of course a novelist, but also the author of a handful of fascinating poems; Nicholas Moore, largely forgotten since the 1940s but who continued to write profusely and who awaits a revival; W. S. Graham, who I represent here by two poems written since his important *Collected Poems* of 1979; Elizabeth Smart, commemorated here by George Barker; and of course Robert Graves who published no poems during the 1980s, but whose influence as poet, critic, novelist was crucial for the continuation of that alternative tradition to Modernism which connects himself, Thomas Hardy and

Edward Thomas to Philip Larkin and other poets in this anthology.

Robert Graves saw the modern age as one of criticism and consolidation. Certainly the literary criticism and journalism printed in books, the books pages of the weekly, daily or Sunday papers, and poetry or literary journals is complemented by such contemporary critical works as Peter Ackroyd's biography of T. S. Eliot or A. N. Wilson's study of Hilaire Belloc. Modern scholarly editions have led to reevaluations of the reputations of overlooked poets: most significant in recent years are Edward and Alison Lowbury's edition of Andrew Young, Hubert Nicholson's edition of A. S. J. Tessimond, Jean Moorcroft Wilson's of C. H. Sorley, the Bloodaxe Books edition of Hart Crane, and, most important of all to my mind, P. J. Kavanagh's edition of Ivor Gurney.

More proof of the invalidity of Jacobsen's leap up a tree comes from the fine crop of collected poems we have seen in recent years from several generations of contemporary poets. From Roy Fuller, C. H. Sisson, Gavin Ewart, Norman MacCaig, Charles Tomlinson, Michael Hamburger, D. J. Enright, Anthony Thwaite, Geoffrey Hill, Alan Brownjohn, Peter Porter, Michael Longley, James Fenton, Cliff Ashby. In addition three very different books of selected poems must be singled out as key influences on poetry today: John Ashbery for his eclectic and discursive meditative line; John Fuller for the formative influence his stylishness and artistry have had on many of our younger poets; Tony Harrison for his metrical virtuosity and vivid evocation of contemporary themes in the high style.

There has also been a change of heart among many publishers of contemporary poetry. Publishers are trying much harder to sell poetry books through the application of sophisticated marketing techniques and promotions. Century Hutchinson, Chatto & Windus, Faber & Faber, Secker & Warburg, have increased print runs, lowered prices, designed new and often startling covers; some have even sent poets around the country by train, helicopter, aircraft to attract press attention. Penguin Books has launched a new series of collections by poets from Geoffrey Hill to U. A. Fanthorpe. The subsidised presses, such as Anvil Press Poetry, Bloodaxe Books, Harry Chambers/Peterloo Poets, Carcanet Press have promoted their new books just as enthusiastically and successfully.

But these publishers would hardly market poetry in this way if they did not have a corresponding awareness that their books had much to offer more readers; so we must focus on the poems, not the distribution network, to find what is perhaps characteristic of English poetry in the 1980s so far. One way to do this is to locate some of the more memorable individual new books of recent years: Derek Mahon's *The Hunt by Night* (1982), Ted Hughes's *River* (1983), Michael Hofmann's *Nights in the Iron Hotel* (1983), Geoffrey Hill's *The Mystery of the Charity of Charles Péguy* (1983), Seamus Heaney's *Station Island* (1984), Douglas

Dunn's *Elegies* (1985), Hugo Williams's *Writing Home* (1985), Paul Durcan's *The Berlin Wall Café* (1985). The only quality these books have in common is the good poems they contain – as diverse as the individuals who write them – readable, original in conception, yet simultaneously extending and reinventing a live tradition. The health of poetry always depends on the individual good poems written which speak for us rather than the movements or manifestoes which aim to tell us what poems *should* be. Certainly the main impression obtained from the poems in this anthology is of variety and diversity of form and theme. A poem today may be written on any subject under the sun: from Ken Smith's ongoing sequence 'The House of Green Ginger' based on his experiences as the first fellow in creative writing to H. M. Wormwood Scrubs Prison ('Green Ginger' = Wormwood); or Fred D'Aguiar's poem spoken by a night nurse from his sequence on attitudes to mental nursing expressed by those involved; to, say, Michael Hulse's honest irritation with poor Daria, James Berry's powerful moral tale, Frank Ormsby's poem from his sequence on sport; the diverse meditations of Alan Brownjohn, Philip Larkin, Peter Levi; the autobiographical variousness of Tony Harrison, Seamus Heaney, U. A. Fanthorpe; and the diverse evocations of peopled or unpeopled places from Jeremy Hooker, Ted Hughes, Derek Mahon, Charles Causley. There is humour, too, in a variety of subtle tones from Wendy Cope, Ian McMillan, D. J. Enright; and diverse attitudes to writing on love from Carol Ann Duffy, Gavin Ewart, Tony Curtis, Ted Hughes. There is the passionate formalism of Dick Davis or Robert Wells, and there are portraits of the contemporary scene from Graham Greene, Philip Larkin, Peter Porter. And so on. Poetry today simultaneously entertains, teaches, impresses with its many shapes on the page but, most important of all, continues to express the deepest thoughts and feelings of us all.

My reading of poems from magazines and new books over recent years (including two pleasant years as a PBS selector) has also convinced me of a renewed sense of Coleridge's esemplastic power of imagination in contemporary poetry. Imagination is of course essential for any good poem: a force by which the poem *lives* for both writer and reader, but there does seem to be a marked amount of it in many of the poems gathered here in a variety of ways. From B. C. Leale's surrealist fantasy, or Terence Heywood's expressive imagery, both of which open doors onto strangenesses; to Michael Hamburger's dream poem, or the mystery and sheer authority of Ted Hughes who has done much to encourage experiment in poetry today and free it from pragmatism; to the very different, yet complementary shapely inventions of John Fuller or Norman MacCaig. Among the better known younger poets, the contrasting imaginations of Craig Raine and Jeremy Reed as seen here are instructive too: the former communicating a precise sense of wonder and freshness, the latter with his eye firmly on the specific elements of a particular landscape. Other elements of imagination are present in the compressed narration of Blake Morrison's poem on a secondhand car lot (Morrison, with Andrew Motion, has rehabilitated the longer narrative poem too in recent years), Gillian Clarke's windmill which 'knocks stars from their perches', Charles Boyle's authentic picture of Lincolnshire viewed from a bicycle saddle; or Ron Butlin's elliptical narratives (Butlin in many ways is the most directly lyrical of the younger poets): and then there is the technical confidence and attack in the poems of Michael Hulse and Peter Reading, both ready to tackle situations or emotions unfamiliar to much poetry.

Most noticeable of all, though, must be the imaginative invention of the newest generation of poets to whom language expresses things on several levels simultaneously. Exceptional and daily life, ideas, things seen or felt, even the transcendental, are vividly made concrete for the reader in their poems. It is not easy to pinpoint what has shaped their various styles. Certainly Michael Hofmann, Michael Hulse, Stephen Romer, James Lasdun, Ron Butlin, Jeremy Reed, Oliver Reynolds would seem to be well aware of modern European writing as well as British. Perhaps also the American poet John Ashbery whose poetry acknowledges that the world contains many realities, many truths, viewable from a variety of viewpoints depending on who is observing. Additionally, the Modernist poet from the past to whom they are nearest in spirit is surely, if anyone, Wallace Stevens (himself an influence on Ashbery), master of subtle nuance and the poem as object in which thought and emotion merge into feeling intellect. These poets are alike only in the way they invent the poem wholeheartedly, unselfconsciously, with intelligence and intellectual energy. They are confident that the inner world of imagination, far from evading reality, in fact leads immediately back to the outer world of public, personal and political events. They restate the importance of the individual inner life as counterbalance to the contemporary dominance of the public life we must all share, perhaps to teach us better what E. M. Forster meant by his phrase "only connect".

Come on back down to earth out of that tree, Jacobsen, and read on. Things are not as they seem. These poems are for you too.

Jonathan Barker

The Ocnophil and the Philobat

Distant the city lights. Now at nightfall
I imagine writ above this ruined door
that opens to a blackness which descends:
'Visitor, discover Nothing here. Endure.'
I dreamed that once and still the words pursue.
I wouldn't go down there if I were you.

I had another dream the other night:
slopes of snow; standing figures cut from ice,
shaped like Henry Moores. They seemed to threaten,
they dragged behind them, blurred and imprecise,
shadows owning a red or purplish hue.
I wouldn't go down there if I were you.

Stone balustrades wind round into the dark
and I drop a stone. So long before it lands.
You remark, 'I'd like to see what lies below,'
and nonchalantly offer me your hand
although the roof above is all askew.
I wouldn't go down there. I wouldn't . . . Careful!

Still you insist and beckon me to come
and childlike shout, 'I dare you. Take a chance,
the more we experience the more we know
and the more we journey into ignorance.'
Agreed, but there are doors I'll not go through.
I wouldn't go down there if I were you.

GEORGE BARKER

In Memoriam E.S.

Ah most unreliable of all women of grace
in the breathless hurry of your leave-taking
you forgot – you forgot for ever – our last embrace.

PATRICIA BEER

The Footprint

A small patch of sand has lain –
It is never less than whole –
For years now, month in month out
On the grey promenade, blown
Through a gap in the sea wall
By a wind with wrecks in it.

The first bare foot of summer
Stepped there this morning, the print
Heavier than all the shoes
Of winter. Did the swimmer
Shake off the sea as he went
Inland to his sunlit house?

The sea will catch up with him
When summer is gone. The wind
Will bring yellow poppies in
From the sand dune and pin them
On to firs. No one will find
His footprint ever again.

His house will creak as bell-buoys
Ring from the estuary,
Gales will put salt into fresh
Water. There will be a noise
Like doomsday as the sea
Hits him with a storm of fish.

ANNE BERESFORD

The Question

He looked up
his book still in his hand,
that dazed expression
so well known
saddened her.

But, he did look up,
looked through her
out to the window,
the garden, robin perched
on japonica – briefly.

She spoke into the void
of his mind – or hers –
'Not again, never.'
Nothing moved
even outside nothing stirred.

'Understand, I can't
explain it more.'
Again the silent afternoon
the fear on her neck.

And slowly she watched
his eyes move slowly back
the book trembling – briefly –
in the heat.

JAMES BERRY

Offenders

The sea swallowed my son.
I was stung; my genius was stung.
I worked.
I worked to drain oceans.

Then fire charred my friend
and set me ablaze inside.
It took my time.
It took my time beating down flames.

Then air poisoned my wife.
I invented space.
I rounded up air.
I imprisoned air without rest.

Land slid and buried my lady.
I swung.
I swung flattening hills.
I flattened hills nonstop.

Then my thumb stabbed my eye.
One blow cut my thumb clean off.
Now, see, both my hands
are mere butt ends of a rifle.

CHARLES BOYLE

Cycling in Lincolnshire

There's my bicycle standing
under a dripping tree, open country
behind and the rain coming down
in silver spokes. . .

You could believe the earth was flat,
bounded by a sea with a Latin name.
Wild man Tennyson
scuttled along the hedgerows,

leaving a trail of damp red herrings:
birdsong, and the insistent jingle
of an ice-cream van touting for custom
in the New Town estates.

Once, staying bed and breakfast
in the middle of nowhere, I shared a room
with a Chinese mature student
who took his presence there for granted.

I preferred sleeping rough in barns.
Sometimes, the farmer's wife
would bring me hot milk,
and would stand in the open doorway
watching me drink it too fast –

                    Next morning,
I'd leave at dawn: a keen recruit
in the resistance movement.

ALAN BROWNJOHN

In January

In the salt-marshes, under a near black
Sky of storm or twilight, the whole day
Dark on the creeks where the wind drives wavelets back
Against the filling tide, I have lost my way

On a path leading nowhere, my only guide
The light halfway up a television mast
Five miles across the waste; and if I tried,
I could imagine hearing, under this vast

Raw silence of reeds and waters, the deep drone
Of generators, gathering up the power
To send its message out; and, stopped alone
By this channel's edge, revisit a lost hour

At a restaurant table, in a vanished place
(An organ chiming in the hushed cave below)
When three sat smiling in an alcove space
And saw their futures, thirty years ago. . .

And ten years earlier, learn each adverb clause
Written out in the spring by those in dread
Of School Certificate; without much cause
For fearing death as long as they had read

The good green textbooks. Further back, next to me,
Her pencils in a leather pouch, her dress
A blur of gentle yellow, is a she
Who smiles with such a sidelong vividness

I can even touch her hand. And further still,
I walk up between desks rising in tiers,
And see the old imperial pictures fill
The walls of the same room, lit by gasoliers

— My father's now. Then suddenly return
To the path over the marshes, and the light
On the meccano mast, which tries to burn
As strongly as a fixed star, secure and bright

Against the black of nightfall; and provides
Small quizzes for our lounges, puppets that grin
To tame the evening's terrors. England hides
Its head in its small comforts . . . Seeing in

— Alone and lost and darkling — this New Year,
I stare round at the dark miles of this nation,
And through the winter silence only hear
The loveless droning of its generation.

RON BUTLIN

An Incident in Paris

A light was burning in a room across the street.
In the flat next door a clock chimed thrice:
three forty-five in the ninth arrondissement,
27th August 1985.

Nearness was cutting into me like glass
lacerating every sense and nerve,
until the darkness that I stared into
was clear, transparent –

A room in Paris: a dressing table, a carpet
and matching curtains, make-up, clothes, a bed,
the girl I'd met earlier that evening.
In her the night-sky and the certainty
of love seemed briefly indivisible:
silence falling into place around us
and inside us.

Afterwards I glanced across the street;
the light had been switched off. The clock began
to strike: I was healing too quickly.

RON BUTLIN

The Story of a Life

Once when he was young he reached into the fire
from longing to possess the colours there.
That moment's red and faltering yellow drew
the substance of his pain into
itself. Thirty years passed.

Today he's practising piano, a Chopin waltz.
A neighbour's dog starts barking – so
he hammers even harder, *con fuoco*,
on the keys. Lunchtime drunks join in;
an out of tempo siren passes clawing
at each phrase. Meanwhile, two floors below,
ghetto-blasters measure out the bass,
the dead are thrust into their rightful place.

He is the fire he reaches into now,
he grasps at flames and burns. As one
by one the colours that were his return,
briefly the interrupted story is resumed.

CHARLES CAUSLEY

The Prodigal Son

I could remember nothing of the village:
Only, at a sharp elbow in the lane
Between the train-station and the first cottage,
An August cornfield flowing down to meet me;
At its dry rim a spatter of scarlet poppies.

I had forgotten the cement-botched church,
The three spoilt bells my grandmother had christened
Crock, Kettle and Pan; the cider-sharp Devon voices,
The War Memorial with my uncle's name
Spelt wrongly, women in working black, black stockings,
White aprons, sober washing lines, my Bramley-
Cheeked aunt picking blackberries in her cap,
The butcher's cart, the baker's cart from Chudleigh,
From Christow, and the hard-lipped granite quarry
Coughing up regular dust under the skyline.

But this came later. I heard as I climbed
The white flint lane the still-insistent voices:
'Never go back,' they said. 'Never go back.'
This was before the fall of corn, the poppies.

Out of the sun's dazzle, somebody spoke my name.

GILLIAN CLARKE

Windmill

On the stillest day
not enough breath to rock the hedge
it smashes the low sun to smithereens.

Quicker than branch to find a thread of air
that'll tow a gale off the Atlantic
by way of Lundy, Irish Sea.

At night it knocks stars from their perches
and casts a rhythmic beating of the moon
into my room in bright blades.

It kneels into the wind-race
and slaps black air to foam.
Helping to lower and lift it again

I feel it thrash in dark water
drumming with winds from the Americas
to run through my fingers' circle

holding the earth's breath.

Penelope

No, I wouldn't have chosen this life –
As a young girl I couldn't have faced
Two decades of being a wife
Who must wait and be faithful and chaste.
Though solitude's not to my taste
And nightly I curse him for leaving,
It isn't entirely a waste –
It's awfully good for my weaving.

Now suitors and schemers are rife
In this house that his presence once graced
And I need to be sharp as a knife
And I fear he may never be traced.
When I long to be kissed and embraced,
I remind myself what I'm achieving.
No need, dearest love, to make haste –
It's awfully good for my weaving.

Envoi

My Prince! You shall not be replaced
By another. I'll go on believing
That true love must not be disgraced –
It's awfully good for my weaving.

TONY CURTIS

Midnights

An ice wind from the east razors across
the water, heaves and slams up our road. All night
our windows flinch and rattle with bitter complaints,
for hours the roof lifts and the attic breathes.

In the morning the last of our apples lie
bounced and bruised beneath the trees,
our front cherry's bare as a plucked chicken,
leaves downed across the lawn, its carcass full of sky.

A handful of slates, as old as the century
have snapped and slid to crash the sloping
panes of the verandah – slivers and blades
of glass in the flower border like dew glistening.

I bend for an hour over the job, filling
a bucket with needles, jags and shards.
This evening the weather man promises calm,
explains, last night's storm was brewed in Poland,

a wind from Warsaw chilling across the continent to
                                                    Wales.
We hold to each other now
and listen to nothing but midnight
taxis speeding out of town.

As I stroke your arm
a glass sliver still in my finger
bloodies the two of us.
The windows' thin moonlight fails.

FRED D'AGUIAR

from The Bedlam Papers

iii
Night Nurse

If like me you are seated here
Last-touching the umpteenth version
Of the blasted night report,
So certain X or Y will do
Such and such a thing
That you can count them in,
Zero queuing their need
For a drink, pee, or unofficial
Dose to top-up their usual,
You'd soon come round to my line;
For boredom kills from inside,
Works its way out to the grain
On your face, added, cragged, soured,
Outing the light in your eyes.

I ask little in return, if male,
That they lie on their stomachs
For the three minutes or so
I take riding them flat out,
If female, I lower their heads
To my waist and they understand:
They get whatever they require,
All they have to do is comply.

PETER DALE

Recreation Ground

'Did, Lily dear; did, Lily dear!' of electric told
the halves and quarters, not the pavilion clock;
and the steam-freight huffed the time for home.
The bowling green, a silent movie, rolled
as if slow-motion, underwater; odd chock
and knock like some malfunctioned metronome.

The distant cries of games, it seemed, not fading
but travelling away, diminishing
as if for ever right into the stars
and years away – no illusion, shading
brought on by coming dark – the hollow ring
struck true, and truer now the railing bars

clatter across the carriage-lights of a train. . .
I am reduced once more to a mute boy
gazing at the neolithic corpse,
foetal in its museum pit again,
dreading not death but all the hoi polloi
that, unbeknown, will point with nosy gawps. . .

If it is a land of shades it's where
shadow never falls.
It is sheet lightning overhead
at deep midnight whose glare
calcifies and stalls
time with reiterable dread.

Terror, in any thoroughfare,
random as pigeons round
the tread. . .
And he curled in the great armchair,
eyes closed, to see how near would sound
the distant cries of life to the long dead.

Skin, like charred paper, bound his head.

DICK DAVIS

Here Come. . .

Here come the stragglers and strugglers,
The dropouts, dervishes and jugglers,
The dross whose cases get referred,
Dreck on whom judgement's been reserved.

Here comes the smart-arsed human race
Strutting as if we owned the place.

DICK DAVIS

With Johnson's Lives of the Poets

He wrote these quick biographies
To be instructive and to please;
    In them we find

Among judicious anecdotes
The apt quotation that denotes
    A taste defined,

Abstracted from the record of
His irritable, captious love
    For failed mankind –

From fear, from his compassion for
Insanity, the abject poor,
    The world's maligned.

He laboured to be just, and where
Justice eluded him his care
    Was to be kind.

Read generously – as once he read
The words of the indifferent dead.
    Enter his mind.

CAROL ANN DUFFY

Miles Away

I want you and you are not here. I pause
in this garden, breathing the colour thought is
before language into the still air. Even your name
is a pale ghost and, though I exhale it again
and again, it will not stay with me. Tonight
I make you up, imagine you, your movements clearer
than the words I have you say you said before.

Wherever you are now, inside my head you fix me
with a look, standing here whilst cool late light
dissolves into the earth. I have got your mouth wrong,
but still it smiles. I hold you closer, miles away,
inventing love, until the calls of nightjars
interrupt and turn what was to come, was certain,
into memory. The stars are filming us for no one.

ALISTAIR ELLIOT

At Sea

for Amanda

Lying beside you, shadowed by the jenny
All morning, genially talking in the rubber
Boat on the foredeck – it's how the landlubber
Imagines sailing: cream, in a great vee
Unzipping, which we draw across the sea,
And blue, broken by dolphins for a while
And (fluttering at the bosom of a sail)
Perhaps a lost emigrant butterfly.

Our lifeboat sags, and we bump pleasantly.
In five nights I'll be reckoning at the wheel
The heights of seas – could we untie that boat
Before we sink? – how long could swimmers float
Among these soft ravines? – can this be real? –
Trapped among particles of reality.

ALISTAIR ELLIOT

A Case of Identities

Needlepoint Park: in the Utopia
I've just begun my bacon and home-fries
And eggs, I'm squinting at my newspaper,
When this black man starts giving with the eyes.
He's more than friendly, in this rugger shirt,
And calls, 'It's *Different Strokes*, right?' Like a dope,
Slowly, I see he isn't trying to flirt –
He thinks I'm someone in a TV soap.
Too bad I'm not. And maybe I should do
His number and be Mr Drummond, once. . .
But then I notice he's like someone too:
The oval face of a Nigerian bronze.
   I stare and stare. But it would not be cool
   To tell this stranger, now, he's beautiful.

D. J. ENRIGHT

Poetry Readings

These are very meaningful, for the public can learn
How the poet imagines the words are pronounced and
Which are the ones that actually matter.
Moreover there is always a chance that while thinking
Or drinking he (or less commonly she) will fall off
The platform, or dissolve into self-induced sobbing.
Or at least flirt flauntingly with an attendant mistress
Who of course is beautiful, attractive and farouche
(In the words of Louis Simpson); and probably under
                                                                                  age.

Unless, as may happen, the public is utterly ignorant
Of this significant and rewarding event, since
The organizers have omitted to make it public.
In the grip of passion, the secretary and the treasurer
Have fled clandestinely to the nearest watering-place.
Or the committee has removed to some distant hostelry,
Leaving a notice nailed to the door: 'Mr X is sick',
And applying the travelling expenses to improper uses.
Or quite simply and innocently the date was misprinted.

No skin off your nose if (as Simpson the poet reported)
The Latter-day Saints are rising in an adjacent chamber,
Or a celebrity from Assisi by the name of Francis
Is on stage round the corner with performing animals,
Or the Old Fire Station Arts Centre has gone up in
                                                                                  flames.
Such misfortunes can be borne with fair equanimity.
More likely that while you were making your journey
A blizzard was predicted, and the prudent stay indoors,
Or among 'the many keen admirers of yours hereabouts'
Only two are about, two of the less admiring.
When Mr Y was there, they tell you, the place was
                                                                        packed,
Loudspeakers were erected in the street outside.

Yet always there is someone present, one who deters you
From calling it a day and taking the night train back.
Not the cultivated couple who offered accommodation,
But a woman proclaiming 'I am the Laureate of Leigh-
                                                    on-Sea',
Or a man who has always loved your poem called 'Crow'
Or a book you once wrote whose title, he remembers,
Was to do with a number of types of ambiguity.

For there is no case on record when no one at all turned
                                                    up.
Not as yet.

GAVIN EWART

Lovers in Pairs

Hearing the other one breathe
is a function of all paired sleepers
   and it's coupled with the wish
   such breathing should not stop.

Young lovers lay ears on hearts
and say how it would be ghastly
   if the beating faded down
   to silence — just gone away.

They think the end of the one
would be love's end, for no other
   ever could be the same.
   Of course, they're right — and wrong,

for many will come to the beds
and twenty is different from thirty,
   as sentiment's middle age
   moves slowly and coolly on.

When old ones lie side by side
what's real at last has a look-in.
   The breathing *could*, surely, stop —
   and with it the warmth of love.

It's the penultimate bed
before the one with a gravestone.
   This is what each one thinks —
   a thought sad, loving, and warm.

U. A. FANTHORPE

'Very Quiet Here'

(Picture postcard of Aldeburgh sent by Thomas Hardy
   to his sister, Kate Hardy, on 11 May, 1912)

for Bill Greenslade

In Wessex no doubt the old habits resume:
Fair maidens seduced in their innocent bloom,
May-month for suicide, and other crimes
(Two Dorchester murders discussed in *The Times*),
Mutilation of corpses, infanticide, rape,
And so many reasons for purchasing crepe.
All stirring at home. But here vacancy reigns;
I have nothing to watch but my varicose veins.

    Very quiet here.
Not an apprentice has perished this year.

I envy Crabbe the matter that he saw:
Those wasting ills peculiar to the poor,
Decline and dissolution, debts and duns,
The dreary marshes and the pallid suns —
So much for him to write about. And I
In Wessex homely ironies can spy.

    None of that here.
Even dear Emma a trifle less queer.

Deck-chaired and straw-hatted I sit at my ease,
With each blighted prospect determined to please.
Inside my old skin I feel hope running on —
Perhaps a changed life when poor Emma is gone?
Strange foreknowings fret me: guns, music and war,
A corpse with no heart, a young Briton ashore
Walks here where I sit with the atheist Clodd,
Discussing the quirks of that local cult, God.

    I ponder how
Time Past and Time to Come pester me now.

U. A. FANTHORPE

At Averham

Here my four-year-old father opened a gate,
And cows meandered through into the wrong field.

I forget who told me this. Not, I think,
My sometimes reticent father. Not much I know

About the childhood of that only child. Just
How to pronounce the name, sweetly deceitful

In its blunt spelling, and how Trent
Was his first river. Still here, but the church

Closed now, graveyard long-grassed,
No one to ask in the village. Somewhere here,

I suppose, I have a great-grandfather buried,
Of whom nothing is known but that, dying, he called

My father's mother from Kent to be forgiven.
She came, and was. And came again

To her sister, my great-aunt, for
Her dying pardon too. So my chatty mother,

But couldn't tell what needed so much forgiving,
Or such conclusive journeys to this place.

Your father, pampered only brother
Of many elder sisters, four miles away,

Grew up to scull on this river. My father,
Transplanted, grew up near poets and palaces,

Changed Trent for Thames. Water was in his blood;
In a dry part of Kent his telephone exchange

Was a river's name; he went down to die
Where Arun and Adur run out to the sea.

Your father, going north, abandoned skiffs for cars,
And lived and died on the wind-blasted North Sea shore.

They might have met, two cherished children,
Among nurses and buttercups, by the still silver Trent,

But didn't. That other implacable river, war,
Trawled them both in its heady race

Into quick-march regiments. I don't suppose they met
On any front. They found our mothers instead.

So here I stand, where ignorance begins,
In the abandoned churchyard by the river,

And think of my father, his mother, her father,
Your father, and you. Two fathers who never met,

Two daughters who did. One boy went north, one south,
Like the start of an old tale. Confusions

Of memory rise: rowing, and rumours of war,
And war, and peace; the secret in-fighting

That is called marriage. And children, children,
Born by other rivers, streaming in other directions.

You like the sound of my father. He would
Have loved you plainly, for loving me.

Reconciliation is for the quick, quickly. There isn't
                                                    enough
Love yet in the world for any to run to waste.

JOHN FULLER

A Sudden Hail

Once again it is up and over
The stone stairs, parabola
Of ascent for its own sake.

Such climbing is a kind of entry,
Keeping at a distance like
A courtly petitioning.

Laboured breathing is the guilt of a
Restless creature captured by
The supremely immobile.

The head is lowered and eyes are raised
In deference to altitude
At its purest, crest on crest.

At the top the sky starts to open
Like the drawing of curtains,
Fine veils, a theatre scrim.

And an attic hail sprinkles on moss
A careless largesse, cloud stuff,
The hand of the jeweller.

Up and over: the giant presence
Of what, when we are conscious
Of it, becomes endurance,

Something to be lasted that is there
Still when we find it will not
Last, and looms behind us like

The cruel deliberate legends
Of a mountain race for whom
The sky is really a god

And whose future falls like the seasons
On a receptive landscape,
Short shadows, too soon cut down.

We know it is scattered at random.
We know it is our brief gift
Like the snow's lifted waters,

Like the hail's rough milky diamond
Resting a moment against
The tiny feathers of moss.

After that it is all a downward
Tread, tread on tread, the loud heart
Lifted frankly like a face

That attends to its ordinary
Business in a warm valley,
Living cries, level dealing,

And for whom weather is common talk
With other faces and is
That delight faces can bring.

The Life and Death of King John

In my old age I disremember why
I got the volume down. Perhaps to check
My memory of the lines (no more than two)
I uttered in the part I played at school.
I think in those ancient days I merely knew
Act IV, Scene I, though that by heart, despite
My only being First Executioner.
What curious turns the mounting years have brought!
'When we were happy we had other names.'
Unlikely then I would have noted lines
So apropos oneself; or even those
With general resonance, such as the Queen's
'A strange beginning: "borrowed majesty" ' –
Seeming to comment on some work of art.

And in such times of peace and empire I
Would anyway have seen as commonplace
'That white fac'd shore . . . that water-wallèd bulwark.'
Today a great historic frisson comes:
'King Richard Coeur-de-lion was thy father.'
I never thought to feel England in my person –
Decline, and lingering greatness, chance of cure;
Honoured by John's more sapient successor.
Though must have made out how congenial
The Executioner's love of legality
And sentiment (if not his cowardice):
'I hope your warrant will bear out the deed'
And 'I am best pleas'd to be from such a deed.'
I often think: ' 'Tis strange that death should sing.'

W. S. GRAHAM

The Visit

How would you like to be killed or are
You in disguise the one to take
Me back? I dont want to go back
As I am now. I'm not dressed
For the sudden wind out of the West.

Also sometimes I get lost.
If I stay on for a bit and try
Upside-down to speak and cry
HELP ME, HELP ME, will anything
Happen? Will I begin to sing?

What a fine get-up you have on,
Mister, if that is your entering name.
How did you get through the window-frame
To stand beside me? I am a simple
Boy from Greenock who could kill

You easily if it was not you.
Please tell me if you come on business.
You are too early. I have to kiss
My dear and another dear and the natural
Objects as well as my writing table.

Goodnight. I will mend the window.
Thank you for giving me time
To kiss the lovely living game.
So he went away
Without having touched me.

He looked at me with courage.
His head was a black orange.

W. S. GRAHAM

Look At The Children

Look at the children of the world
Looking out at us to say hello
All from their lonely photographs.

Look at the children in their year
Which they know nothing about.
What lovely round big eyes they have.

What's to be done? What's to be done?
The hungry dogs are come to town.
Where have your father and mother gone?

Look at the children of the world
Appearing in the newspapers
Not knowing we are here at all.

The thing is they are beautiful
Because of something maybe not
A mystery all that deep.

Look at them looking out at us
Not knowing we are making an obscene
Use of them. They are all lovely

Enough for us to take home to the soul.
And who would you choose? The difficult one
With the not straight left eye looking?

Look at them. Why are they not seeing us?
The thing is they are beautiful
Not knowing us, in spite of us.

Look at the children of the world
Breaking our hearts but not enough
While we eat our money up.

GRAHAM GREENE

World War Three

It was at best a small affair,
I had never heard of the island,
I had no intention of dying there
For a people I didn't know.

The radio talked of a greater affair,
Moscow gone and London destroyed,
I had to patrol the island there
For a people I didn't know.

The war I knew was a small affair,
I had never heard of the island,
I died of a snake bite in the bush
For a people I didn't know.

GRAHAM GREENE

Go-Slow

It was go-go-slow at Clapham Junction,
it was go-slow by the clock,
yet how swift the hours that I waited there
would have seemed to the man from the dock.

I was one of a crowd on the centre platform,
while three hours passed on the clock,
but no one bothered to notice me there
as they'd noticed the man from the dock.

The longest go-slow at Clapham Junction
was half an hour by the clock,
when they laughed at Wilde as he waited there
in handcuffs fresh from the dock.

GRAHAM GREENE

The Outsider: On the Death of
Adlai Stevenson after
a Press Conference in London
on the Vietnam War

Tiredness can resemble dishonesty,
and when he spoke to us,
it was only a matter of minutes
before the tired heart stopped.

So we were amazed by the words he used—
'We shall always fight against an outsider
imposing his will,' he said.
'Who is the outsider?' we demanded,
but he gave us no reply.
For tiredness can resemble dishonesty,
and you must be very tired when you die.

The outsider was waiting,
on the Embassy steps, in Grosvenor Square—
the outsider who is always finally there,
even though you begin
with an advantage in tanks and guns
and a 7th Day Adventist fleet;
the defences fall and the outsider steps within
and death resembles defeat.

MICHAEL HAMBURGER

Endless

It began as a couch grass root,
Stringy and white,
Straggling, to no end,
Branching out, breaking
For procreation.

Traced and pulled, it became
A bramble shoot that climbed
Through leafage of shrub, tree
With a root at its tip, for plunging.

I pulled at it, pulled,
Miles of the thing came away,
More and more.

I pulled and pulled until
I saw that now
Straight up it had risen
With its end in space,
With a root in heaven.

TONY HARRISON

The Morning After

I
The fire left to itself might smoulder weeks.
Phone cables melt. Paint peels from off back gates.
Kitchen windows crack; the whole street reeks
of horsehair blazing. Still it celebrates.

Though people weep, their tears dry from the heat.
Faces flush with flame, beer, sheer relief
and such a sense of celebration in our street
for me it still means joy though banked with grief.

And that, now clouded, sense of public joy
with war-worn adults wild in their loud fling
has never come again since as a boy
I saw Leeds people dance and heard them sing.

There's still that dark, scorched circle on the road.
The morning after kids like me helped spray
hissing upholstery spring-wire that still glowed
and cobbles boiling with black gas-tar for VJ.

II
The Rising Sun was blackened on those flames.
The jabbering tongues of fire consumed its rays.
Hiroshima, Nagasaki, were mere names
for us small boys who gloried in our blaze.

The blood-red ball, first burnt to blackout shreds,
took hovering batwing on the bonfire's heat
above the *Rule Britannias* and the bobbing heads
of the VJ hokey cokey in our street.

The kitchen blackout cloth became a cloak
for me to play at fiend Count Dracula in.
I swirled it near the fire. It filled with smoke.
Heinz ketchup dribbled down my vampire's chin.

47

That circle of scorched cobbles scarred with tar's
a night-sky globe nerve-wrackingly all black,
both hemispheres entire but with no stars,
an Archerless zilch, a Scaleless zodiac.

TONY HARRISON

The Effort

'The atom bomb was in manufacture before the first
automatic washing machine.'
Tillie Olsen *Silences*.

They took our iron railings down to dump
on Dresden as one more British bomb,
but Mam cajoled the men to leave a stump
to hitch the line she hung the washing from.
So three inches didn't end in German flesh.
It was the furthest from surrender when she flew
a rope full of white Y-fronts, dazzling, fresh
from being stewed all day with dolly blue
in the cellar set-pot. Her ferocious pride
would only let quite spotless clothes outside.

Washes that made her tender hands red raw
we do nowadays in no time by machine.
No one works so hard to keep things clean
so it's maybe just as well she'd got to die
before the latest in bombardments and before
our world of minimum iron and spin dry.

SEAMUS HEANEY

from Clearances

I

A cobble thrown a hundred years ago
Keeps coming at me, the first stone
Aimed at a great-grandmother's turncoat brow.
The pony jerks and the riot's on.
She's crouched low in the trap
Running the gauntlet that first Sunday
Down the brae to Mass at a panicked gallop.
He whips on through the town to cries of 'Lundy!'

Call her 'The Convert'. 'The Exogamous Bride'.
Anyhow, it is a genre piece
Inherited on my mother's side
And mine to dispose with now she's gone.
Instead of silver and Victorian lace,
The exonerating, exonerated stone.

II

Polished linoleum shone there. Brass taps shone.
The china cups were very white and big–
An unchipped set with sugar bowl and jug.
The kettle whistled. Sandwich and teascone
Were present and correct. In case it run,
The butter must be kept out of the sun.
And don't be dropping crumbs. Don't tilt your chair.
Don't reach. Don't point. Don't make noise when you
                                                    stir.

It is Number 5, New Row, Land of the Dead.
Where grandfather is rising from his place
With spectacles pushed back on a clean bald head
To welcome a bewildered homing daughter
Before she even knocks. 'What's this? What's this?'
And they sit down in the shining room together.

III

When all the others were away at Mass
I was all hers as we peeled potatoes.
They broke the silence, let fall one by one
Like solder weeping off the soldering iron:
Cold comforts set between us, things to share
Gleaming in a bucket of clean water.
And again let fall. Little pleasant splashes
From each other's work would bring us to our senses.

So while the parish priest at her bedside
Went hammer and tongs at the prayers for the dying
And some were responding and some crying
I remembered her head bent towards my head,
Her breath in mine, our fluent dipping knives –
Never closer the whole rest of our lives.

VI

In the first flush of Easter holidays
The ceremonies during Holy Week
Were highpoints of our *Sons and Lovers* phase.
The midnight fire. The paschal candlestick.
Elbow to elbow, glad to be kneeling next
To each other up there near the front
Of the packed church, we would follow the text
And rubrics for the blessing of the font.
As the hind longs for the streams, so my soul. . .
Dippings. Towellings. The water breathed on.
The water mixed with chrism and with oil.
Cruet tinkle. Formal incensation
And the psalmist's outcry taken up with pride:
Day and night my tears have been my bread.

TERENCE HEYWOOD

Supernova

However frequent peaks in Darien,
Denmark's without – a modest hillock or two,
Not to be laughed at (it's the only Danish
Thing that one doesn't). So the day that Tycho
Brahe was walking in the abbey grounds
At Heridsvag, and stopped astounded, had
Acres of flatness for astonishment
To burst upon: A new star, really?
He doubted his own eyes. No, he was right,
Some workers going home assured him. Off
Straight to his uncle's study he reported:
A new star in the firmament: one gasped
And wondered: stars were fixed, eternal. What
New age was dawning?
                         His, (so time began
To show). Tycho's astronomy
Was centered on his star: 17 months
He studied it, star table and a copy
Of Ptolemy's collected works on hand,
He studied it until it disappeared.

De Stella Nova was his book, with tables
Of observations: Scandinavian
In diligence, precision, phlegm, about
This new, this newfound thing. From foundering,
Astronomy outgrew astrology,
Revived and flourished. Famed astronomer
Was given a Baltic isle: Uraniborg
Rose and detained him. Kubla Khan had come
To northern waters.
                         How the island was
Swapped for an emperor's castle is another
Tale. . .

MICHAEL HOFMANN

Don John of Austria

(for F. and S.)

The population kept changing downstairs: single women,
unmarried mothers, whole families of petty criminals. . .
A former Miss Austria lived in a pub
round the corner. Old women managed hens
and vegetable gardens, and walked parallel to the ground.
The powerful Herr Briesnigg came to cut the grass
once a fortnight, his hair cropped closer than Bismarck's,
a cigar between his lips, and his square fingers
lubricating the throats of a couple of beer bottles
like a couple of thirsty women.

Afternoons were swingtime. I followed the tuba's
                                        trochees,
the jolly military gambollings, the *pom*pom ostinato
on every single song Frau Kräuth ever played. . .
The flat afternoon sunlight left a spectrum on my wall
                where it bled from the cut glass of a lamp.
One sister went with a boy who offered her violence
(once he knocked himself out against a wall), the other
with her maths teacher, a calculating, durable heart-
                                                throb.
Her white flared jeans were cut like cocktail glasses,
so tight, they were attended by gynaecological
                                        complications.

Summer and winter,
I walked through the maize-field,
six feet of feed-crop or six feet of snow.
I told skinny blue-eyed Gerda I was partial to her,
but her schoolmarmish mother, a vigilant divorcee,
wouldn't have it. . . She was too innocent –
a fellow-member of the Alpine Flower Society
gave her a baby. At night,
the single chalk-white beam of a searchlight
went up over the airport, crying to high heaven.

In ten years, I never learned the names of the streets.
There were half a dozen yellow rubble churches,
a statue of a dragon and a clubman,
some safe clothes-shops. The only amenity
was Mini Mundus, world-famous buildings waist-high. . .
My mother's preferred cobbler knew no lost causes.
Herr Fuiko repaired everything, he had a gold cup
for men's shoes, and a silver one for ladies.
Bernhard Bauer, my sister's best friend's brother,
was junior mini-golf champion of all Austria.

The one window of opportunity was the glazed, blasé
noticeboard where the Catholic press sat in judgment
on Westerns and Italo-Westerns, porn and home-grown
                                        comic porn.
They all came alike to the censor – and to my father
                                        and me,
who went to practically everything with decent
                                action. . .
In the trailers you could see what you were missing,
like the corners of Happy Families cards. Breathtaking –
while our man was getting stuck in the heart-shaped hole
in the shutter, or trying the wrong window altogether,
a woman was picking over dildoes like a box of
                                chocolates.

JEREMY HOOKER

from Itchen Water

Itchen Navigation

What I love is the fact of it.

A channel kept open, shipping
stone for the cathedral;
blue Cornish slates;
coal from Woodmill
to Blackbridge wharf.

A channel used, disused,
restored, until the last barge
passed under the railway bridge,
now abandoned, framing
water that is going nowhere,
but silts, with passages
the colour of stonedust
and boys rowing, a surface
silver and boiling
where blades dip and turn.

It is the stillness
afterwards, grey water
settling back to the shape
of slow working journeys
during a thousand years.

TED HUGHES

Lovesick

You barely touched the earth. You lived for love.
How many loves did you have?
Was there even one?

Or you just loved love.
Love, they say, meaning Dante's God,
Which has a sense in heaven – on earth, none.

Or Love, meaning biology: gene tactics
Of the reproductive system:
Faceless, mindless, almost the fire in the sun.

The Sun
Is its own Aztec victim, tearing for food
Its own heart out, eating only its own.

What was your love? Eyes, words, hands, rooms,
Children, marriages, tears, letters
Were merely the anaesthetics – the lulling flutes
As you fed your heart to its god.

No matter what happened or did not happen

You burned out. You reserved nothing.
You gave and you gave
And that included yourself and that
Was how you burned out
A lonely kind of death.

TED HUGHES

Devon Riviera

Under the lingerie of the August evening
The prepared resort, a glowing liner,
Leans towards happiness, unmoving.
The whole vessel throbs with dewy longing.

Grey, dazed heads, promenading their pots,
Their holiday shirts, their shrunk, freckled forearms,
With hobbling wives who look more like their mothers,
Smell rejuvenation in the ebb.

And lard-thickened ex-footballers, with their high-
                                       tension scowls,
Trailing headache wives and swollen kids
Towards another compulsory steak and chips
Sniff the beery skirts of liberation.

Mauve-dusted, balanced pairs of spinsters,
Walking to interest an appetite,
Venture their compass-delicate stomachs
Among guffaws and squeals and gaping perfumes.

Decent couples, rigid with loneliness,
Expose themselves
Intermittently, with buttoned faces,
To the furnace interiors of fun-halls.

And easy girls from the North, their half-closed eyes
Fixed on the wine-dark sea-haze towards Jersey,
Loll back in cliff alcoves, above the town out-fall,
While waiters from Pisa gnaw their necks.

They see gulls dangling stainless cries
And colliding for tossed-up fish-guts
Above my chugging boat
That nudges happily home, through the purple,

Hauling the rich robe of sewage.

MICHAEL HULSE

Washerwomen at Würzburg

In cotton polka dot and check
the washerwomen work in line
on the scrubbed and scoured and barren deck
of a washboat on the Main.

Thick-ankled, heavy-hipped, they bend
to wash the daily dreck away.
Dirt of the living, world without end:
tomorrow is another day.

Thirty-nine or thereabouts,
the photograph. The river flows
as time requires. Whatever doubts
it washes with it no one knows.

MICHAEL HULSE

Fire

A rage of flame, and even
the green wood begins
to keen and whine,

the sap
bubbles and blisters and browns:
this is the meaning of burning,

the limbs and the blood
blackening into heat. I watch, and worship
with the ardour of a heretic.

MICHAEL HULSE

Daria at the Krümel

Never – if
you're honestly concerned
about my peace of mind –

never ever set me up again
with a blonde one tenth as dumb
as Daria. Ukrainian,

I might have known: half an hour
of anti-Russian small talk, then
Are you religious? Do I breathe?

Patiently,
as if by speaking carefully and clear
she'd get her message over,

Daria described
her guardian angel, her constant sense
of his presence, how

he whispered the word she'd forgotten
in a translation test. *What
was the word*? I asked. *Provocative*

she said. This seemed unpromising.
I asked her how she knew
her angel was a he.

Some things you simply feel she said.
Don't you agree? Beyond the steamy glass
a tram trundled through the snow

and people I would never know
passed, laughing, agreeing there are
certain things you simply feel.

JENNY JOSEPH

Another Story of Hare and Tortoise

There was something I forgot to tell you when I told
                                        you the story
Of the hare and the tortoise. You remember,
How the one animal, splendid, desirable, eager
Life tingling in its limbs, was admired by all
And how the other
Arrived when nobody was actually looking.

They said it was his desire to win – obstinacy.
Nobody else was there. He said he got there.
We were all gathered round the starry hare
Succouring his weakness.
(His faint was only a lapse; he was a splendid runner).
But even if it's true what tortoise said
We were not there to greet him at his win.
The world had gone elsewhere
We wanted to be with hare.

The loneliness of saying 'I won' to nothing but emptiness!
He was not liked. He worked for what he got
And always so damned fair.
It was much more fun with hare.

JENNY JOSEPH
from Extended Similes

Shawls

We walked in the garden as day lifted the sky and here and there on the dark hedges lay white patches, fine wool stuff soaking wet with droplets that made them seem shrunken pieces of fallen mist, like little bits of out-of-place snow still solid when the field round it is warm and green again, finest fairy wool stuff pieces spread to whiten under the dry moon and caught by the danks and darks of night.

Only close up did you see the thousand threads of the fabric, large cobwebs visibly engorged by the wet on them.

It was as if shawls of the lightest wool, the softest merino had been placed here and there, delicately with no pressure, no weight on tired bones, as when the gentleness of love puts with a light touch a fine scarf round frail shoulders, baby-soft fabric nestling up to gossamer wisps of white hair.

Some gentle love had floated down these drifts, these shawls of dew and they remained there undisturbed on the dark evergreens well into the clear day.

PHILIP LARKIN

Modesties

Words as plain as hen-birds' wings
Do not lie,
Do not over-broider things—
Are too shy.

Thoughts that shuffle round like pence
Through each reign,
Wear down to their simplest sense,
Yet remain.

Weeds are not supposed to grow,
But by degrees
Some achieve a flower, although
No one sees.

PHILIP LARKIN

Success Story

To fail (transitive and intransitive)
I find to mean *be missing, disappoint*,
Or *not succeed in the attainment of*
(As in this case, *f. to do what I want*);
They trace it from the Latin *to deceive*. . .

Yes. But it wasn't that I played unfair:
Under fourteen, I sent in six words
My Chief Ambition to the Editor
With the signed promise about afterwards –
I undertake rigidly to forswear

The diet of this world, all rich game
And fat forbidding fruit, go by the board
Until – But that *until* has never come,
And I am starving where I always did.
Time to fall to, I fancy: long past time.

The explanation goes like this, in daylight:
To be ambitious is to fall in love
With a particular life you haven't got
And (since love picks your opposite) won't achieve.
That's clear as day. But come back late at night,

You'll hear a curious counter-whispering:
Success, it says, you've scored a great success.
Your wish has flowered, you've dodged the dirty feeding,
Clean past it now at hardly any price –
Just some pretence about the other thing.

PHILIP LARKIN

How

How high they build hospitals!
Lighted cliffs, against dawns
Of days people will die on.
I can see one from here.

How cold winter keeps
And long, ignoring
Our need now for kindness.
Spring has got into the wrong year.

How few people are,
Held apart by acres
Of housing, and children
With their shallow violent eyes.

PHILIP LARKIN

Aubade

I work all day, and get half drunk at night.
Waking at four to soundless dark, I stare.
In time the curtain-edges will grow light.
Till then I see what's really always there:
Unresting death, a whole day nearer now,
Making all thought impossible but how
And where and when I shall myself die.
Arid interrogation: yet the dread
Of dying, and being dead,
Flashes afresh to hold and horrify.

The mind blanks at the glare. Not in remorse
– The good not done, the love not given, time
Torn off unused – nor wretchedly because
An only life can take so long to climb
Clear of its wrong beginnings, and may never;
But at the total emptiness for ever,
The sure extinction that we travel to
And shall be lost in always. Not to be here,
Not to be anywhere,
And soon; nothing more terrible, nothing more true.

This is a special way of being afraid
No trick dispels. Religion used to try,
That vast moth-eaten musical brocade
Created to pretend we never die,
And specious stuff that says *No rational being
Can fear a thing it will not feel*, not seeing
That this is what we fear – no sight, no sound,
No touch or taste or smell, nothing to think with,
Nothing to love or link with,
The anaesthetic from which none come round.

And so it stays just on the edge of vision,
A small unfocused blur, a standing chill
That slows each impulse down to indecision.

Most things may never happen: this one will,
And realisation of it rages out
In furnace-fear when we are caught without
People or drink. Courage is no good:
It means not scaring others. Being brave
Lets no one off the grave.
Death is no different whined at than withstood.

Slowly light strengthens, and the room takes shape.
It stands plain as a wardrobe, what we know,
Have always known, know that we can't escape,
Yet can't accept. One side will have to go.
Meanwhile telephones crouch, getting ready to ring
In locked-up offices, and all the uncaring
Intricate rented world begins to rouse.
The sky is white as clay, with no sun.
Work has to be done.
Postmen like doctors go from house to house.

The Two of Them

Their lives are turning into gold. The door
Bristles with brass, its own commissionaire –
A valedictory hand swims up
Through metal as I grasp it, then the glare
Of summer spills like lacquer on the floor.

I step inside. A domed clock's pendulum
Taps out a rally. Under glass, the spring
Visibly unwinds. It's like a body
Flayed open for its soul, where everything
But the invisible, heartbeat-beaten drum

Of time itself is shown . . . Their rooms withhold
No secrets; I deduce the two of them
From every corner – even a window box,
The alchemist in the tulip stem
Transmuting earth to shells of glassy gold;

They're in this sheen, from mornings when I'd watch
One of them brush the zodiacs of dust
From varnished wood, the yellow cotton's dark
Reflection rising, brightening, till just
As it was turning into gold, the touch

Of its own substance snuffed it out . . . Sometimes
I find them in the garden, gin in hand,
The fizz still showering upward through the glass,
While insects brush their skin like sprinkled sand
And lazy fingers spin a bowl of limes –

Summer evenings . . . silence like a sheet
Pockmarked by a sound, beyond the wall,
Like a giant clock – and once or twice a night,
A golden, almost luminous tennis ball
Drops from the dark blue, bounces round our feet,

A compact imp that skitters on in fun,
Idling to a halt at someone's chair,
And then it's like a chill, and I imagine
Arriving to discover no one here,
The two of them now one of them, now none.

JAMES LASDUN

Twin Towns

Anywhere is better than here:
Hakluyt and Mandeville, seeking the arcane
'Vegetable Lamb', the diamond nourished on dew
Or fleet one-footed Ethiopian,
Were not more curious than these who rise
On endless escalator waves
To try the London rain on nordic tongues –

Anyone is better than us:
They stare as if I were England emerging at last
Like a fish coaxed from its weeds in the aquarium
Where they have stood for hours in watery tedium –
I catch one blond-lashed eye, then flicker past.

B. C. LEALE

Because the Night

because the night had been swept clean of dreams
taxis were full of the towering
smoke of opals
swerving from the avalanching stones
of Rouen Cathedral
that fell silently out of the iris of Monet's glass eye
for clocks on stilts were blowing about in a high wind
& words were crawling from the pages of books
& a violent ocean in the manner of Hokusai
brandished its prickly foam
in tightly corked bottles
because the night had been swept clean of dreams

because the night had been swept clean of dreams
candles were being lit in the spectral vaults of whales
armed guards were removing their hats from refrigerators
& placing shrill-voiced wineglasses in the burning ruins
of their febrile heads
at the geometric approach of reason
for termites thrived only in kingdoms of phallic earth
& mirrors were being repeatedly struck by the angry
fists of women
demanding back the incredible beauty of their youthful
faces
as Hieronymus Bosch signed his name
with the bloodless leg of a spider
because the night had been swept clean of dreams

PETER LEVI

5.20 and 5.21

5.20 and 5.21,
the dawn is coming up, and village lights
begin to glimmer back at the sunlight:
the sleepless mind has comfort, the soul sings.

5.20 and 5.21,
the evening curtains hang like sky-pillars,
and the clock is the measure of pleasure,
the wireless and the whiskey and the dark.

But the minute that time is understood
the metal clock is ticking in the blood,
we are losing eternity and God.

NORMAN MacCAIG

Crew

Three men are pulling
at the starboard oar,
the man I am and was
and the man I'll be.

The boat sails
to blind horizons.
Who's pulling on the portside oar
that keeps our course straight?

Pull as we may
we're kept from turning
to port or starboard by that
invisible oarsman.

NORMAN MacCAIG

Buzzard Circling

The landscape wheels round
its centre – the buzzard that sees
a hill slide sideways,
a field spin round.

The buzzard wheels
round another, invisible centre,
the black hole that waits
for buzzard and hill –

that will suck in
all circumferences
to the place that was
before chaos was created.

IAN McMILLAN

Cracking Icicles in Totley Tunnel

Into the dark tunnel
from the white hills
the train slows, almost
stops.

Across the aisle
a man cups his eyes
against the dark window.

I do the same. Peer.
Ice. Heavy, almost marble, solid, almost
alive ice.
Growing ice

cracking and rumbling on the roof.

But we are regular travellers,
we are used to such warnings

in the dark tunnel
under the white
and constant hills.

The train slows, almost
stops; then

begins to go faster
as the ice is broken,
at the end of resistance
we rush into darkness

like a van
speeding from
a fenced-in printworks,

like a fenced-in bus
speeding from a pit.

DEREK MAHON

Achill

im chaonaí uaigneach nach mór go bhfeicim an lá

I lie and imagine a first light gleam in the bay
  After one more night of erosion and nearer the grave,
Then stand and gaze from a window at break of day
  As a shearwater skims the ridge of an incoming wave;
And I think of my son a dolphin in the Aegean,
  A sprite among sails knife-bright in a seasonal wind,
And wish he were here where currachs walk on the ocean
  To ease with his talk the solitude locked in my mind.

I sit on a stone after lunch and consider the glow
  Of the sun through mist, a pearl bulb containèdly
                                                fierce;
A rain-shower darkens the schist for a minute or so
  Then it drifts away and the sloe-black patches disperse.
Croagh Patrick towers like Naxos over the water
  And I think of my daughter at work on her difficult art
And wish she were with me now between thrush and
                                                plover,
  Wild thyme and sea-thrift, to lift the weight from my
                                                heart.

The young sit smoking and laughing on the bridge at
                                                evening
  Like birds on a telephone pole or notes on a score.
A tin whistle squeals in the parlour, once more it is
                                                raining,
  Turfsmoke inclines and a wind whines under the door;
And I lie and imagine the lights going on in the harbour
  Of white-housed Náousa, your clear definition at night,
And wish you were here to upstage my disconsolate
                                                labour
  As I glance through a few thin pages and switch off
                                                the light.

73

BLAKE MORRISON

Nunhead Motors

A dipping wire of fairy-lights sways
In the wind outside the second-hand lot
As a clattery trade-in pulls up in a blaze
Of Simoniz laid on to disguise the daylight
Through the bumper, the dents touched up with spray,
And the turning back of the mileage gauge
To a time before the crap in the ashtray
Overflowed like a salad of old age.

But at night the lines of cars inside the yard
Have the sadness of cattle at a bidding-gate,
Frost-skinned and big-eyed, silent as the guard
Dealing hearts to himself over a stove-light,
The low-burning patience of this lot
Everything will work out if we just wait.

FRANK ORMSBY

from The Sports Section

One Saturday

I

Nose close to the handlebars, bum in the air
like Scobie Breasley,
I'm home from Maguire's betting shop in time
for starter's orders.

Sweet Little Volga Boatman is the one
my father's modest hopes are riding on,
a shilling each way.
                    Speechless since his stroke
suddenly he trails a rein of saliva.
If his legs would take the strain
he'd be skelping his buttocks the length of the home
                                                straight.

II

And a beast, some humped blackness, heaves its head:
the ox in Uttoxeter finding form at last
in troubled light on a Saturday afternoon.

III

Before the commentator's *how they finished*, before he
                                                can slow
to word-pictures of an enclosure,
I'm in the saddle again, away at full stretch
to collect our winnings.

But carrying now the weight, the dead weight
of that baffled mobility.

PETER PORTER

Paradise Park

It is a time of the distancing of friends,
Of quarrels between the possible and impossible,
Of a face thrust at yours calling itself honest,
Of complex words outfacing polysyllables
Shouting through darkness to grey Menschenhass:
Now the sun is setting on the Great Divide
And there is nothing to do and nowhere to hide.

The New has been made and the afterwork sparkles
On barbicans of tenderised cement;
First Worlds and Third Worlds are equally fatigued
Importing and exporting barely describable butterflies
And alloys of the perfect miracle: trade goes on
Beyond Apocalypse and the dying and the hopeless,
Hurdles of misrule leapt lightly by the press.

It is also a time of renunciation, of the artist,
That master of paradox, becoming invaluable
By giving up hope, of his escaping his egotism
By abandoning his art. And who will notice,
Among the lengthening queues for Retrospectives,
A sacrifice so slight it moves no pivot's sliver
On warning systems in the nocturnal silver?

For, despite Doomwatch and its calibrated fright,
The human creature is forever coming into
Its inheritance, and out of little towns making
Famous hats and from stevedoring fastnesses
On unsavoury rivers, provincial hopefuls
Arrive at the capital, saving for The Weekend Ark,
The Violent Prater, the sails of Paradise Park.

You may sit at glass-topped tables with white wine
Or play the board games with commanding titles –
Conspiracy Theory, Life Support, The Pursuit of the
                                        Millenium –

76

But nobody gives up early, there is always a smile
Just behind the carousel's blind horse which hints
That being born is coming into pleasure and so who
Is waiting out there for you to be unfaithful to?

PETER PORTER

The Vogue for Despair in Manchester, Rusholme

Perhaps it was the cold or ceaseless rain,
the unfamiliarity along a road
where takeaways sit opposite
drenched parks and civic galleries,
cement escarpments which might be
corporation car parks or schools of music,
'Sweet Houses' with their neat pagodas
of green and lilac cubes on shelves of glass,
betting shops with greyhound silhouettes
and horse shapes doing knees-ups –
perhaps the unfamiliarity was familiarity
wrenched a little to nudge the self to know
it was away from home, wherever
that might be: to follow shining tyres to town
to enjoy Pre-Raphaelite husbandry
nestled among the shopping fortresses,
rain still flicking at the skin like tears –
the end was a despair
so prophetic it could write on walls
'The city has a face, the poetry
of fear. It waits for hope.
Elsewhere apples of temptation grow
among the castled grass and rainbows
of exaggeration. The human soul
is like a shattered windscreen;
what once was clear is sugared now
on pavements. So stretch the suburbs of unease
where pictures tell no stories and the rain
like the neighbours is always at the windows.'

CRAIG RAINE

Heaven on Earth

Now that it is night,
you fetch in the wash
from outer space,

from the frozen garden
filmed like a kidney,
with a ghost in your mouth,

and everything you hold,
two floating shirts,
towels, tablecloth, a sheet,

ignores the law of gravity.

Only this morning,
the wren at her millinery,
making a baby's soft bonnet,

as we stopped by the spring,
watching the water
well up in the grass,

as if the world
was teething.
It was heaven on earth

and it was only the morning.

PETER READING

Aeolian

Trollies marked Kwik Save poke wheels and baskets from
thick-frozen slurry massed in the paddle-pool;
    their wires, wind-twanged, zither. Coke cans'
      light alloy clackily rolls on chimed ice,

stuttering, blown, tintinnabulant: ——/—ᴜᴜ/——
—ᴜᴜ/—ᴜᴜ/—// [Bleakly harmonious grot.]

PETER READING

S. rusticola

Flushed from meshed rust and ginger dead bracken and
bramble, a woodcock, russet-barred, uncalling,
    swishes, explodes up, plumply zigzags.
      Underfoot: oval of steaming cupped stalks

faintly imprinted in frost-silvered leaf-mould, fecal sac
                                 still warm,
chestnut-edged buff wisp of down. . . instants of tangible
                                         loss.

JEREMY REED

Going

At Hill Farm, a downslope spread
    of creeping thistles untamed by a hoe,
a colony well rooted, cows would tread

a cluster flat in the meadow,
    but leave no gap that root buds wouldn't close.
A purple spike of plumes, a finch would show

a flash of pink, yellow or black
    alighting in a fixtured coronet.
Another field showed thistles in a stack,

rooted out, spiny for a fire,
    prickly as holly, more gregarious.
Two or three cows gaped over the barbed wire

of a field fence, that amber day
    I found the pappi silvering, white-haired
patriarchs, it was the still had them stay,

a puff of breeze, and they would fly,
    downy parachutes, light as gossamer,
luminous seeds snow-blown across the sky.

I stayed on, a glitter shook free,
    the air was squadroned with their drifting heads,
featherish stars flaking an alder tree.

I watched them going, a blizzard
    misting the valley, their random touch-down
would colonize fallow, hedgerow or yard,

their uplift varied with the wind,
    some had blown over the hill-ridge and left
clusters of headless thistle stalks behind.

OLIVER REYNOLDS

From the Irish

There's a head by Blake
with wingspan eyebrows
of a man who taught him
'Painting &c
in his Dreams'.

Waking now like Jonah
in a room ribbed with dark
I find your face persists,
a fearful smeared grey
crying success and failure.

My throat cracks,
the mouth struck open
on hollowed breathing:
dumb gusts
in the small cave.

Last Ash Wednesday
we read together in Dublin
in Buswell's downstairs bar,
our table and chairs
backdropped by a door

marked GENTLEMEN
and our poems saluted
at quarter-hour intervals
by the urinals
sputtering applause.

Off the airport bus
by the bookshop (a Kavanagh
first edition for 60 punts)
and the kids begging silver
on the Halfpenny Bridge,

I'd seen two men
with soft cindery moles
on their foreheads.
Coincidence, I'd thought.
Or brothers.

STEPHEN ROMER

The Master in Italy

His thought is chaste as a eunuch
though not unstirred by the baroque

Ecclesia di Gesù, a lusty baritone
and an opulent young nun.

Indiscretions! To walk in Rome
without an overcoat, and countenance boredom

as an elegance in the young,
though it isn't quite done

to preen in bar mirrors or recline
in the Pincio for a whole afternoon.

Supreme badinage. . . But leave him in the evergreen
fatigue of a dusty villa garden

and he rinses his reader
of approximate despair

by weighing the cornices
of actual light, and speaking sentences.

STEPHEN ROMER

Les Adieux

Irrevocable: *Hic Incipit Vita Nuova*.
He takes his leave of her forever

in a final screed. Nobilities of farewell
invent a style

enriched with sacrifice and melodrama.
He sends it and his mind is calmer,

jaw set firm, books and baggage packed.
His own man now, he's free to act,

breathe deeply and respond. . . Three days later
a relapse: a second farewell letter

from a German spa. The water
did not obliterate her,

and by this time letter number one
will have been received, perused, forgotten.

Which is why he must fervently renew
(this last time) his final adieux.

STEPHEN ROMER

Confiteor

Your will has shrunk to a small thing now, limp
with self-pity, the creeping damp

that favours fungus and discolour.
Mind has its own attractive squalor,

wet rot, dry rot, an ineradicable dream
it would bankrupt you to wake from.

You're half in love with what destroys a house
by undermining it, dislodging the mortise

from its tenon. Grown careless of the love
that built it, and of the trove

beneath it, your notions of rectitude
have peeled away, replaced by crude

silent images, or a fixed illusion
who is beautiful and leads you on

to a lit piazza or an olive grove
pink on silver, a far remove

from where you are.
Persist, and you may learn the horror

of estrangement in your house, the unconcealed
knowledge of it in the new eyes of your child.

CAROL RUMENS

Digging

For Seamus Heaney, from Surrey

In this sub-culture of gardens
one who avoids weedkiller
might well be hung from the tallest
ornamental cherry:

but, if I'm hooked, it's simply
a lei flung over my shoulders
to welcome and shame me
as I home to my graveyard patch.

I knew if I looked too long
I'd fall in love with flowers.
Their tender vividness,
helplessly self-parading,

catches my breath as if
they were my own daughters
pursing their lips to paint
the sharp little shadows and brighteners

into too-candid glances.
I bow towards the soil,
and unshawl the first damp babies
— lobelia, kitten-faced pansies.

I don't understand what they want
or what they silently know.
Are my fingers making them cry?
All afternoon I'm at sea

in photosynthesis.
I tell the time wrong
by the unusual sun.
Half my life has passed;

I should be digging elsewhere.
Yet still my hand, obsessed,
grips the blunter tool,
says: I'll write with it.

KEN SMITH

from The House of Green Ginger

For the Lost Boys, Sleepless

The usual sniggering on the stairs,
and from the night park the shrill
peacock scream might be rape or mankilling,
pierced rat or some tortured innocent.

No one calls the cops. I don't.
The night somehow goes on, whatever riddle
the owl alone in wet rainy leaves
knows the answer to. I don't,

don't sleep or awake each night dream
the same black, the same trains
made up in the yards, last word
of a late argument, the door slammed.

In the House of Green Ginger

Where I'm banged up inside as if dreaming
the dream shut tight and I never get out.
In the dark yellow hive I'm in with the bees
where the last man out was a spy for Russia
dreaming of wings on the fourth iron walkway
of D Wing: cell by cell in its socket,
the bolts home early, the smug keys
sleeping it off, the late shift at the spyhole
counts each man alone, and there's no honey.

In my room as it happens I've a view
east over wire and the wind and the wall
to the nurse's home and the city beyond.

CHARLES TOMLINSON

Annunciation

The cat took fright
at the flashing wing of sunlight
as the thing
entered the kitchen, angel of appearances,
and lingered there.

What was it the sun
had sent to say
by his messenger, this solvent ray,
that charged and changed
all it looked at, narrowing even the eye of a cat?

Utensils caught a shine
that could not be used, utility
unsaid by this invasion
from outer space, this gratuitous occasion
of unchaptered gospel.

'I shall return,' the appearance promised,
'I shall not wait for the last
day — every day
is fortunate even when you catch
my ray only as a gliding ghost.

What I foretell
is the unaccountable birth each time
my lord the light, a cat and you
share this domestic miracle:
it asks the name anew

of each thing named
when an earlier, shining dispensation
reached down into mist
and found the solidity
these windows and these walls surround,

and where each cup,
dish, hook and nail
now gathers and guards the sheen
drop by drop
still spilling-over
out of the grail of origin.'

ROBERT WELLS

Epigram

Your god is the one that makes the ears of corn
Milky, when the wind is soft in the field.

Later it will blow over the cracked earth
With a dry shiver that is thirst's own sound.

HUGO WILLIAMS

Deserter

The days hang back. They come at me
in shock-waves, like bad news. They dawn so late
I sometimes think I missed one in my sleep
and lie here counting them. From where I lie
I can see them parading past my window
like soldiers going to war. White curtains
drawn back and forth across my sight
are handkerchiefs in the hands of girls
waving goodbye to their loved ones. See –
they are coming round again, accusing me
with their blood-stained uniforms
of having betrayed them. Motes of dust
revolving in the first rays of sun
are all it takes to make me feel afraid.

DAVID WRIGHT

A Charm

To send you sleep I send you images.

A full moon building a pacific ocean
Your boat floats in the middle of; a world
Of black air and flat water; blind as silence.

A shallow valley below bowing mountains,
A force so far off you don't see it move,
Hung between mountains berried rowans bower.

A Sunday; jacarandas line the square;
Aloes, azulejos, a white church tower;
A nun in sunlight, patient as prayer.

To send you sleep I blend you images.

DAVID WRIGHT

White Christmas

Outside the window, snow that fell
In so large flakes two weeks ago
Recedes, reluctant as the thaw;
The bare, black water of the river
Moves slowly, hardly moves at all.

The disappointment of the year
Reflected in a sky that's clogged
With grey, a woollen sheet of cloud;
All bone and feather, the blackbird.

The longest night's about to fall
Thickening a dead gleam of snow
That upon ground too long, too long
Has lain, and burned the grass below.
On such an evening, Christ be born.